a cartoonist's chronicle

Tyne Bridge Publishing

Acknowledgements

Geoff Laws extends grateful thanks to ncjMedia; Brian Aitken, Editor of The Journal; Paul Robertson, Editor of the Evening Chronicle; Simon Donald; Paul Linford.

Thanks to Peta who over the years did everything that the family needed while I was upstairs hunched over a hot drawing board.

The publishers wish to thank ncjMedia for permission to reproduce those cartoons that were first published in the Evening Chronicle, The Journal and the Sunday Sun.

Our grateful thanks also to Elanders for their support.

ISBN 978 185795 201 8

Published by
City of Newcastle upon Tyne
Newcastle Libraries
Tyne Bridge Publishing
2010
www.newcastle.gov.uk/libraries

www.tynebridgepublishing.co.uk

Printed by Elanders, North Tyneside

For Peta, Anna and Ben

The Queen pays income tax, 1993.

A word from Simon Donald

GEOFF LAWS has, all through his career, produced the best caricatures I've ever seen anywhere, bar none. There's simply no one better at what he does.

The skill of a great caricaturist is a unique gift, and a rare one. People often think, because I spent so many years working as a cartoonist, I must be able to do cartoon likenesses of real people, but it really doesn't work that way. I could no more produce a likeness of Geoff than he could replicate any of my great work, such as swearing on national breakfast television.

Geoff's talent to capture the very character of a person lies in a combination of an eye that sees faces in a unique way, and a hand that has the deftest touch to capture that vision, in an image in which a tiny stroke out of place could ruin the likeness.

We can all be truly grateful that he's chosen to spend his career working in his native Newcastle. Doubtless he could have chosen to work for pretty much any national paper you could name, but Geoff has stayed at home.

A modest and gentle man, Geoff is one of the North East's most overlooked treasures.

I hereby declare this book open! Here's to many more years of stunning artwork from the great man.

Simon Donald

Co-Founder Viz Comic, Author and
Internationally Renowned Toilet Humourist

Bobby Thompson, the Little Waster. **Evening Chronicle, 1986.**
Bobby was presented with the original on one of his many retirements.

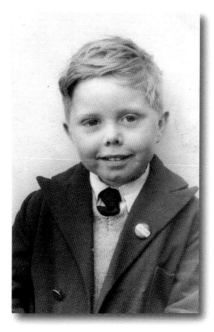

At Bebside infant school in 1952 with an excellent school blazer made from a re-cycled WW2 army greatcoat and monitor badge in lieu of medals.

learning to draw

WHEN I WAS VERY YOUNG we owned one of those big old fairy tale books with separate colour plates. It was Edwardian, a classic period for illustrators like William Heath Robinson, an artist whose work I still love today. We also had Rudyard Kipling's Just So Stories with his own quirky illustrations and later I was given an edition of Treasure Island with the fantastic drawings of Mervyn Peake.

I loved looking at these books and they marked the beginning of my fascination with drawing. Unfortunately they disappeared over the years along with my Meccano set and Davy Crocket hat.

It was in the early 1950s that I first became interested in cartoons. I was visiting my grandparents in their terraced house in Goschen Street, the house where I was born in 1947, in the Cowpen Quay area of Blyth, then a busy port on the coast north of Newcastle.

Every now and then our Canadian relatives used to send over their big fat broadsheet Sunday newspapers. I don't know why. They had entire pages of classic American cartoon strips like Li'l Abner, Blondie, The Katzenjammer Kids and Mutt and Jeff in colour. I enjoyed looking at the strips although I can't have made much sense of the eccentric dialogue and lifestyles they portrayed. I discovered only recently that it was Frank Frazetta, one of my favourite illustrators, who drew the Li'l Abner cartoons at that time. How amazing is that?

In the late 1950s, when I was about ten, and the Suez crisis was in the news, I came across a newspaper cartoon depicting the head of President Nasser as the continent of Africa. He had a plaster on his neck, which in the drawing was stuck over the Suez canal. I was fascinated by the way the cartoonist had not only made a face out of Africa, but had also made it look like Nasser *and* told the story of the blocking of the canal.

I began drawing when I was very young, starting in the pram so I've been told, although I wasn't allowed a knife to sharpen the crayons. The earliest drawings I still have date from when I was six. One is a street scene with flags flying from the lamp posts to celebrate the Queen's coronation in 1953.

When I was eight, having graduated from crayons, I won a painting competition at our church with a watercolour on the theme of washing day. I was taught to do perfect colour washes by my dad, who was an architectural draughtsman and did all his plans in colour. I also inherited drawing genes from my mum, a talented artist.

By the time I went to secondary school I was drawing cartoon faces, seeing how far I could distort them in amusing ways and I spent hours filling sketchbooks.

On a Saturday I would often wander down to Blyth market, past the old woman hand cranking the roundabout and the crowd watching the scary escapologist writhing about in chains inside a scruffy old coal sack. My destination was a yellow trailer with a fold-down side that sold, amongst other things, small format comics about the second world war. I would browse through them until I found what I was looking for, a good artist. Some of the comics had superb atmospheric black and white drawings. I would choose my favourites and spend hours copying them as accurately as I could. Drawing always drawing!

As a teenager I had great fun with my mates in Blyth. We were always laughing with off-the-wall ideas – daft poems, silly songs and cartoons. Regrettably I also enjoyed playing the fool in class. I was the smallest in my year and humour was a way of amusing bullies so they wouldn't pick on me ... I was also a very good runner if humour didn't work.

This behaviour in class led to 'could do better' appearing on my school reports more often than I would have liked and I suffered the consequences when handing over the reports at home. It didn't help that my mum was a teacher. I was often told that if I didn't work harder I would end up at the shipyard or down the pit.

My interest in caricature grew and I spent ages copying the ones in the Radio Times and TV Times. I soon discovered that there was a fine line between capturing a likeness and missing it altogether. I never dreamed that twenty years later I'd be drawing caricatures for the TV Times.

Outside the back of my grandparents' house in Goschen Street. I'm wearing the full Blyth Spartans kit with head numbing leather football and boots with toe caps so wobbly that it was impossible to pass the ball with any degree of accuracy. At least that was my excuse.

When I reached the sixth form at school I progressed from copying caricatures to using live models – the teachers. I drew them during the lessons and nabbed each one in turn. They were then stuck up on the wall in the sixth form common room. At the end of one lesson a teacher, who until then had been missing from the gallery, turned to me and said 'Well, did you get me?' I thought I had been really clever and discreet hiding the drawing behind a pile of books and haversacks!

I was awarded the sixth form art prize in my last year at school, but was denied the pleasure of walking on stage to collect it.

The prizes were given out at the speech day ceremony during the autumn term, by which time I was at college. I returned to school having made the effort to dress up in my best clothes. A blue checked shirt with button-down collar, slim knitted tie, black cord trousers, desert boots and a grey tweedy jacket that buttoned up like a Beatle jacket with a collar. Quite conservative I thought, but not a suit.

It was almost my turn to go up on stage when the Latin mistress noticed me. I saw her frown, then go over to the deputy head who approached me and suggested that my clothes were, to use his words, 'rather *outré*' and I should stand aside from the queue. Quentin Crisp wouldn't have lasted five minutes in Blyth.

When my name was announced I at least had the satisfaction of hearing the accompanying cheer, and I had the last laugh because for my prize I was mistakenly given the hardback version of The Arts of Man (35 shillings) instead of the paper back at 18s 6d. Yes!

Schoolboy cartoons: clockwise from top left, my art teacher, my biology teacher (famous for his rages), and my French teacher.

At art college in the late 1960s, with an attempt at whiskers.

art student

I ENJOYED ART AT SCHOOL because it was the one subject that came naturally to me. My art teacher, Don Green, took an interest in my work and was very encouraging, often exclaiming 'Exshlunt Laws! Exshlunt!' ramming the point home with a stiff forefinger to my chest.

When we talked about where I might go after leaving school the obvious place was art college. Don found out about a new course that might suit me – three-dimensional design. The other options were graphic design, which I didn't fancy because I didn't want to work in advertising, fine art, from which there was no guaranteed way to make a living and fashion design which I wasn't interested in.

3-D design sounded like a fascinating area that might even lead to interesting and lucrative employment. So I applied and was accepted at Newcastle College of Art and Design in 1965.

The course gave a grounding in fine art, the tighter disciplines of graphic design and technical drawing, sculpture and 3-D design as well as an understanding of materials and construction.

There was a distinct hierarchy amongst the students. At the top (in their opinion) were the 'Fine Artists', who went out of their way to look the part with long hair and as much paint on their clothes as on their canvases. Known as 'sweet FA' by the ceramics tutor, they held themselves aloof.

Next were the 'Commercial Artists', destined for the advertising industry. We 'Industrial Designers' came at the bottom of the pecking order and were referred to as 'the scrubbers'.

One of the first classes to challenge us at college was Life Drawing. I remember nervously waiting for the entrance of the model for the first time, not knowing what to expect or how I would react. She walked in, a rather overweight middle-aged woman, dropped her robe, and was soon reclining on an old leather chaise-longue in front of a two bar electric fire while we set up our easels. Once the pose was established the tutor left and, after a period of concentrated drawing, we began to chat. In a while the chatting got a bit loud and the model told us to keep it down. I think we'd woken her up. After her rather abrupt request, a voice from behind a drawing board hissed 'Who does she think she is? Telling us off in the nude!' triggering a splutter of suppressed laughter all around the room.

College work took up a lot of my time so I didn't do many drawings of my own, but I did go on experimenting with cartoons.

I was becoming more interested in the way people looked and the way they wore their clothes. When I went to the pub with my mates in Blyth I used to carry little notebooks so I could do quick sketches of the locals. Sketching like that helps to develop the eye because you have to record things quickly before the subject moves. Considering we've all got the same bits, the variety of the human form never ceases to amaze me.

At college we used Rotring pens for technical drawings. These pens have thin tubular nibs that draw a line of a set thickness and you have to change nibs to change the widths of the line. As I got more familiar with these pens I started to use them for cartoons, beginning tentatively with the very fine nibs. It wasn't until I started at the newspapers that I discovered the old-fashioned dippy-in pens which allow you to draw much more expressive lines.

I use HB pencils on bristol board which is thin card with a very smooth surface. The board will take a lot of rubbing out without roughening, and the pen glides over the surface without snagging and splattering – most of the time!

The pens have the traditional metal quill nibs, are very flexible and I can draw lines from very fine to really thick just by varying the pressure on the board. They also allow you to have splotchy accidents and you can dip your fingers in the ink to dab them around.

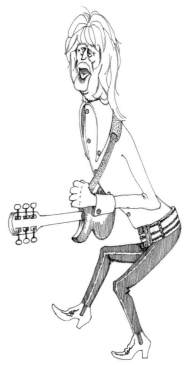

Drawing lines in different directions and layering them gives texture and shading as well as describing shapes and bringing dynamism to the drawing.

I like areas of solid black in my drawings because they add strength and richness and I fill these areas in with a brush. I use a very dense ink so even the finest lines reproduce well. It is also waterproof, which is essential when painting over with watercolour.

What's the most important thing to remember when drawing with pen and ink? Put the lid back on the bottle as soon as you've finished!

In the 60s, our local pub in Blyth, The Spartan, sold a few bottled drinks enjoyed mostly by women. The names of these drinks were ideally suited to the south-east Northumbrian accent so a typical order on a Saturday night might go … 'Sivvin pints uv Ordinrry, a Churrry B for wor lass, fower Snaabaals an' a Powney'.

the summer job

EVERY SUMMER BREAK while at college, I was lucky enough to land a job as a labourer at Blyth harbour. I say lucky because I enjoyed the outdoor work and got to meet some great old characters. I took the opportunity to photograph and sketch some of them during the tea breaks.

Each summer the depth of the river had to be measured to see which areas needed dredging. In its own inimitable way Blyth Harbour Commission's system involved two boats, six people, two reels of wire, a lead weight, two grubby white flags, a notched stick and a tide gauge. The depths were taken from the seaward ends of the piers up to the power station at the north end of the harbour.

The action started when George, the engineer in charge of the soundings, decided that the weather was suitably clement and the water calm enough to have a day on the river. He would ring the harbour yard and two craft, the size of large rowing boats, with a combined crew of five would set off upstream to meet him.

Meanwhile George would walk down to the jetty, near to the harbour office, to set up the tide gauge. Inside a locked cabinet on the jetty was a brass drum round which George would wrap a piece of graph paper. He wound up the mechanism that turned the drum slowly over a period of about twelve hours and fixed an ancient stub of pencil so that it made contact with the paper. The pencil was connected by a series of levers and pulleys down a wooden tube to a float that sat on the surface of the river. As the tide ebbed and flowed the changing height of the river was recorded as an undulating line on the paper.

By the time George had finished setting up the gauge the boats had arrived at the jetty to meet him and off we chugged up the river to the next sounding site. If it was a particularly warm day we would avoid working near the sewage outlets.

Only one of the boats had an engine, with an old harbour hand, Billy, as helmsman. Billy was a slightly built chap, dressed in his brown boiler suit and cap, nervously adjusting his specs as they slipped down his nose. His boat had a big cable drum sitting amidships and the end of the cable would be tied to one of the rings that were embedded in the jetties and walls at intervals along the riverside. The sounding boat, without an engine, stayed there and Billy took his craft across the river paying out the cable behind. He wore an old sack tied round his waist to protect his boiler suit from the cable as it went past. When the boat reached the other side it was tied up to a convenient ring and the two crew members, usually students, wound up the drum until the cable was taut and out of the water.

A grubby white flag on a stick was hoisted on each boat to warn passing ships that the cable was in place. Of course they were totally inadequate as a warning signal, being the size of a handkerchief, and often the cable had to be speedily unwound to allow a ship to pass and prevent the boats being dragged under. I'll never forget the sight of Billy frantically waving a flag in the vain hope that an approaching ship's captain would not only notice him but also do an emergency stop.

Meanwhile, across the river, the sounding boat was manoeuvred, with a single oar (a new skill), to the start of the cross-river

Billy on the alert for approaching ships, ready to wave the grubby white flag on the right. The rest of the team can just be seen in the other boat making their way along the cable.

cable. George would take out his notebook and one of the crew, usually Dick Turpin (brylcreamed hair, blue boiler suit, donkey jacket and wellies; keen on ballroom dancing), would unwind a cable from a reel overhanging the side of the boat. On the end of the cable was a lead weight and when this reached the river bottom a gauge on the reel showed the depth. George entered this number in his book along with the time and I would use a notched stick to pull the boat along the cable stretched across the river. There were lead markers attached to the cable at intervals of ten feet and at each marker another depth was measured.

Dick Turpin in relaxed mood, in charge of the depth gauge, waiting for George to arrive from the office to begin another day's soundings.

Having made the crossing, the sounding boat was hitched to Billy's boat and that was cast off from the jetty. Billy's two crew members then had the job of rewinding the cable onto the drum which pulled everyone back across the river. The cable was released from the jetty at that side and off we would go to the next sounding site.

And so it would go on hour after hour, day after day, week after week, so that, weather permitting, by the end of the summer all the measurements had been taken. It came round every year, creating a job for life!

At the end of the day George was ferried back to the jetty where he removed the graph paper from the tide gauge and took it back to the office. He then had to look at each of his readings and compare them with the height of the tide at the time they were taken. Each reading required a calculation to compensate for the rise and fall of the tide during the sounding operation and from that he worked out the mean depth of the river at each point. Simple!

Oh, and one more thing. There was usually too much of a swell towards the harbour mouth to take accurate depths in the usual way so they sent out the Harbour Master's launch and they did the whole job in about twenty minutes with the echo sounder.

I got £14 a week for that job when beer was the equivalent of around 7p a pint!

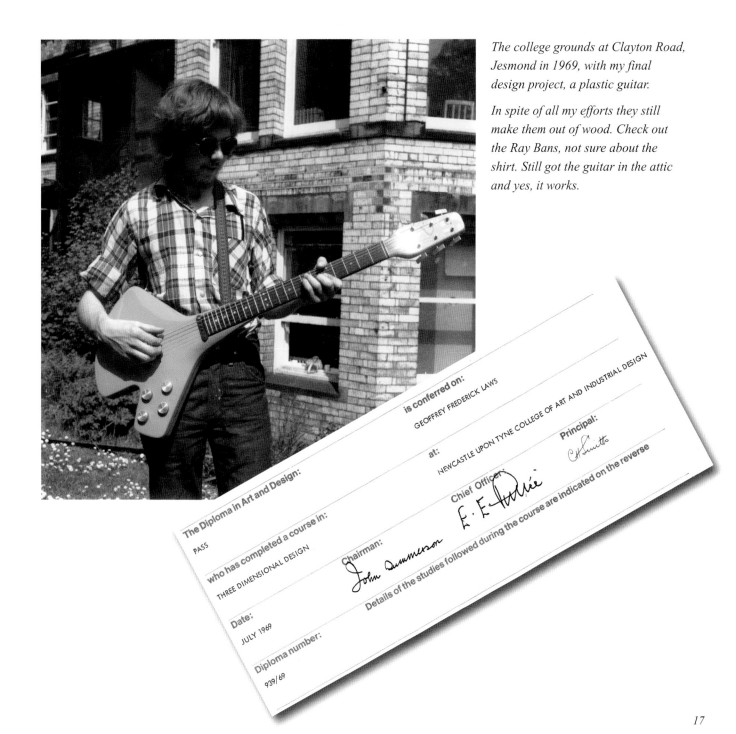

The college grounds at Clayton Road, Jesmond in 1969, with my final design project, a plastic guitar.

In spite of all my efforts they still make them out of wood. Check out the Ray Bans, not sure about the shirt. Still got the guitar in the attic and yes, it works.

The Diploma in Art and Design:

is conferred on:

GEOFFREY FREDERICK LAWS

at:

NEWCASTLE UPON TYNE COLLEGE OF ART AND INDUSTRIAL DESIGN

who has completed a course in:

PASS

THREE DIMENSIONAL DESIGN

Principal:

Chief Officer:

Chairman:

Details of the studies followed during the course are indicated on the reverse

Date:

JULY 1969

Diploma number:

939/69

Filling an idle moment at the flat in Finsbury Park, 1971. I was born too late to be a Ted.

the big smoke

THE 1960S WAS A TIME of great optimism when everything seemed possible, to me at least. Working-class people from humble backgrounds were reaching the top in all spheres of life including fashion, film, music and art. Naturally, the guys at college thought all we had to do was successfully finish the course and we would be set for great things. Reality was slightly different and, out of my year, only one person went on to get a job connected with what we'd studied.

I graduated in 1969, and after labouring once again at the harbour over the summer I was offered the draughtsman's job in the Engineers office. One of my tasks turned out to be converting thousands of those sounding measurements into a huge contour map of the riverbed. The job was pleasant enough but it wasn't going anywhere, so after nine months I decided to leave, at which point I was told that they were about to put me in charge of the soundings. What a missed opportunity!

My next job was with a firm of vehicle body part suppliers called James & Bloom in Shieldfield, Newcastle. I designed leaflets and learned how to work a printing press. They said it was either that or teach a printer how to design leaflets. I had to leave after four months because I couldn't manage the obligatory bacon, egg, sausage, mushroom and tomato stotties that came with the morning tea break.

Employment opportunities in product design weren't looking very hopeful in the North East, so in 1970 I moved to London.

After six weeks on benefit I managed to land a job as a graphic designer with a big American firm of management consultants, Booze Allen and Hamilton International. The job wasn't brilliant, preparing diagrams for reports, but the luxurious office was. Right in the heart of Mayfair, our studio was on the first floor. The french windows, with floor to ceiling velvet curtains, opened onto Bond Street and Burlington Gardens. It was like being on a Monopoly board, and rather impressive for a lad from Blyth.

The windows gave us panoramic views of the busy streets, and celebrity spotting became an amusing pastime. Elton John would often pop into Cartier the jewellers just across the road, and I'd see John Lennon's Rolls Royce turning the corner on his way to the Beatles' Apple headquarters in Savile Row.

One Sunday morning, after working overtime, I emerged from the office into a deserted street, deserted that is except for David Bowie in his full Ziggy Stardust outfit strolling past with two huge minders. I was so taken aback that I didn't even have the presence of mind to ask for his autograph.

I shared my first flat with two friends in Holland Park, a lovely leafy part of the city, just west of Notting Hill where I often found myself in the checkout queue at the local shop with Robin Day and John Cleese. Unfortunately that only lasted for six months as one of the guys moved away and two of us couldn't afford the rent. Finsbury Park, our new home, was a decidedly less salubrious area. (Another Don Green word, 'very salubrious Laws'.)

Luxurious office accommodation in Mayfair with my fabulous parallel motion drawing board.

Relaxing in the kitchen at the flat in Tavistock Road, Jesmond, around 1974.

bringing it all back home

AFTER THREE YEARS, a move to Camberwell, and two burglaries, the glamour of London had dwindled to a daily grind and I was drawn back to the North East, a decision I've never regretted. Years later when the possibility of working in Fleet Street arose I wasn't even tempted. I soon discovered you didn't have to live in London to work for national and international newspapers.

On returning to Newcastle I worked for McAlpines the builders, filing and distributing the architectural drawings on the site for the new Eldon Square shopping centre. It was good to have a job, but I didn't approve of the short-sighted demolition of Newcastle's historic buildings. At that time they were black with dirt, viewed as out-dated and without merit. Fortunately, the destruction that began with T. Dan Smith was halted when the buildings were cleaned and people realised what architectural gems they had in the city.

I had been working for McAlpines for about nine months when the job of Editorial Artist for The Journal, Evening Chronicle and Sunday Sun was advertised, and I applied. An observant aunt had spotted the advert and cut it out of the newspaper for me. What luck!

After two interviews I was offered the job and in April 1974 I started work at the office in the Groat Market. Little did I know that it would turn out to be the perfect job for me and that I would be there for thirty-five years.

On my return from London I rented a flat in Jesmond and my journey to work was transformed from the crush of London's grimy underground to a refreshing bike ride. I've always loved cycling, and zooming down Pudding Chare in the mornings I would arrive energised and ready for work. The return journey gave me time to mull over the events of the day and settle things down. It was only really bad weather that forced me to take the bus.

Blind Man's Bluff was drawn in 1974 as a protest against the demolition of some of Newcastle's historic buildings and the ensuing pollution from car exhausts.

deadlines!

THE WORLD OF NEWSPAPERS has been transformed since 1974. It was all hot metal production, no computers and the incessant clacking of noisy old typewriters. There seemed to be more characterful old-timers in those days and a culture of drinking was accepted from the editors down. The Printer's Pie pub was even part of the building – although there was no connecting door. You could go into any pub round the Bigg Market at lunchtime and you would see journalists from one or more of the newspapers. Sometimes they were actually interviewing someone, the professional boundaries being as liquid as the lunch.

With this level of drinking going on, for many journalists money was tight. Payday was on a Thursday and I was amazed to see the amount of borrowing that took place each Wednesday. When the company tried to stop weekly pay packets and change to a monthly payment directly into the bank there was uproar among those who knew they would be spent up by week three.

At that time the post of Editorial Artist was a new idea for regional papers. At first nobody really knew what I was supposed to do, but, thrown in at the deep end, I was soon drawing illustrations and cartoons to accompany news stories and features, and pretty much everything that appeared on the editorial pages that wasn't a photograph, including logos, graphs and maps. In those days the quality of printing and newsprint was far inferior to what it is now and a line drawing had greater clarity and was often more effective than a photograph.

I often designed logos that involved type and this brought me into conflict with the printers, because this was their exclusive territory. Whenever I needed some type to be set I had to walk past all the compositors working at the roaring hot metal machines, up to the high desk in the middle of the room and present my written request to the guy in charge, I felt a bit like Oliver Twist asking for more.

The printers had a stranglehold on newspaper production at that time with their fiercely guarded 'Spanish' practices (a way of measuring output linked to bonuses and a monopoly on anything to do with type). My initial requests for art proofs were met with a variety of colourful ways of telling me to go somewhere else and multiply. It took several meetings between representatives of the printing and journalism unions before the printers agreed to co-operate and several months before both sides felt relaxed about it.

An early cartoon with Jeremy Thorpe, Edward Heath and Harold Wilson in a fight to win the general election of October 1974. **Sunday Sun, 1974**

I drew my first caricatures, for the Sunday Sun, within a couple of weeks of starting at the paper – Joe Harvey and Bill Shankly in a preview to the Cup Final predicting a 2-1 win to Newcastle. I had to do drawings at very short notice of just about anything in the world, and it was time consuming to search the newspaper library for reference photographs, so I started to create a photo library of my own.

In those days the major photographic agencies sent out hundreds of photos, mainly of celebrities, politicians and sports people to the office hoping that they would be published. But, because a fee was payable if they were used in the paper, most of them were passed to me and I filed them. They were invaluable for caricatures because many were snapped on the street or at functions and provided a great variety of angles and expressions. Magazines were another source of photos, and watching celebrities on TV gave me an insight into how they moved and behaved.

The Journal and Evening Chronicle journalists worked in one big open plan room so there was a good deal of banter. One reporter whose name escapes me now was particularly good at one-liners that he delivered in a very dry deadpan style. A young reporter would walk into the room and fall prey to a succession of lines like…

'That's a nice jacket… *pause…* Did they not have it in your size?'

Then,

'How much did it cost?'

When told,

'Blimey you, could have got a new one for that!'

Short pause, then, in a conciliatory way,

'Do you think that style will ever come back?'

On another occasion as someone enters...

Breezily,

'Hello Tommy, mind you're looking well.'

Pause, then, in a concerned way,

'Have you been bad?'

And when someone was quietly trying to slip away early, loudly across the newsroom,

'Cheerio Bill, thanks for coming in!'

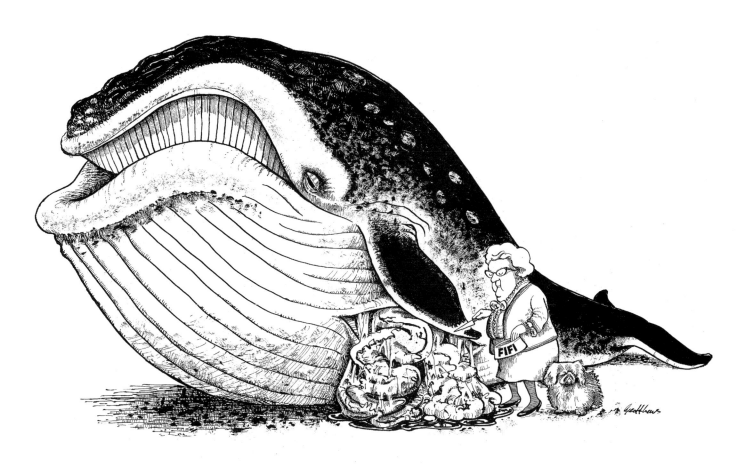

I drew this cartoon in response to the slaughter of dolphins and whales by Japanese fishermen. Thousands of the creatures were being killed every year for exploitation by various industries, among them pet foods and cosmetics.
Evening Chronicle, 1977

learning the art

THE ART OF DRAWING CARTOONS is closely associated with caricature – caricature of personality, expression, attitude and emotion, clothes and props. The art lies in analysing the subject matter and selecting what is important or different. This you grab with both hands and exaggerate, the rest you can ignore.

Working within the tight discipline of a newspaper, where I needed to draw almost anything, usually in a hurry, has been a crucial factor in my development as a cartoonist in terms of technique and style.

Although I was working to tight deadlines, I usually had time to complete complex drawings to my satisfaction, but that wasn't always the case. For the Evening Chronicle first edition, I might have just half an hour to do a full colour cartoon before it was whisked away still wet from under my brush.

I love the drawings of Ronald Searle (though I've never been able to emulate his loose spontaneous lines), and Gerald Scarfe's amazing 1960s drawings were an inspiration. I'm also keen on the work of American Mad magazine cartoonists Jack Davis and Mort Drucker, and the amazing paintings of Sebastian Kruger, but my biggest influence in my early newspaper years was Wally Fawkes (Trog). When I started I would often look at his drawings to see how he dealt with cartoon and caricature problems like fitting large heads on little bodies and particular pen and ink techniques like cross hatching. I admired the clarity and clean lines of his drawings, which although full of detail weren't muddled, and his use of solid blacks, because no matter how much you cross hatch, solid black is richer. It was a great moment when I got to meet him at a cartoon awards lunch. Unfortunately he declined my offer to swap drawings. I don't blame him!

In 1980 the Cartoonists' Club of Great Britain decided to make a big event of their annual cartoon competition with an awards ceremony at the Café Royal in London. I submitted some caricatures and was amazed and excited to receive an invitation to the awards ceremony. I was even more amazed and excited to come second to Wally Fawkes, my all-time caricaturing hero (with Jeremy Thorpe, conspiracy to murder trial 1979). In 1981 I submitted again and was made Feature Cartoonist of the year with a Ronald Reagan caricature (on page 28). Then the following year I was runner-up Feature Cartoonist with a drawing of Cyril Smith (on page 29).

After the 1981 lunch I got talking to Reg Smythe, the creator of Andy Capp, and we travelled back on the train together. During the rather boozy journey he told me about how he worked. He would sit at a table and set his

alarm clock to go off after twenty minutes. During this time he had to think of an idea for a cartoon and draw it. Then he would reset the clock and start again. The following year we shared an exhibition at the DLI Museum in Durham.

Unfortunately the cartoon awards came to an end after 1982, but, because of the publicity surrounding them, my work came to the attention of the Daily Mirror and Sunday Mirror for whom I did many caricatures of politicians throughout the eighties using the pen name Starling. Around that time I also had caricatures published in the Radio Times and TV Times.

The 1980 Cartoonists' Club of Great Britain lunch in the wine cellar of the Café Royal. The tables were full of famous cartoonists, and celebrities like Barry Humphries, Jilly Cooper and Beryl Reid. I got to sit next to an off-licence manager from Hounslow.

The scandal surrounding the trial of Liberal Party leader Jeremy Thorpe concerning the attempted murder of his alleged former lover, Norman Scott (and the shooting of Scott's dog) ruined Thorpe's political career in 1979.
Evening Chronicle, 1979

US President Ronald Reagan as an ageing cowboy.
Evening Chronicle, 1980

This drawing of MP Cyril Smith was once described as looking like 'a vast Christmas pudding with ambulatory facilities'. I liked the idea of him slowly sinking into the car's back seat. But he still has the shifty sideways stare of a politician – no reason to spare him that, though it's nothing personal.
Evening Chronicle, 1981

tv faces

I STARTED TO DRAW CARICATURES for the Saturday TV page of the Evening Chronicle, the Sunday Sun, then every day for The Journal. This continued until I left The Journal in 2009. To start with the drawings were nearly all in black and white with only the occasional one in colour. Then in 1989 new colour presses were installed in Thomson House and the proportion of colour pages gradually increased.

Barrie Humphries, Dame Edna, a caricature of a caricature and a gift to draw.
Evening Chronicle, 1982

Astronomer Patrick Moore. Personal props such as moustaches and glasses are very important. One of Patrick Moore's eyes is just a slit then there is the more obvious look of a seventeen-stone sack of potatoes round his waist, and a telescope of course.
Evening Chronicle, 1984

Ronnie Barker and Ronnie Corbett
Evening Chronicle, 1985

Tommy Cooper **Evening Chronicle, 1983**

Woody Allen **Evening Chronicle, 1983**

Warren Mitchell **Evening Chronicle, 1985**

The Royal family at Christmas, watching the Queen's speech. **Evening Chronicle, 1985**

Bruce Forsyth **Evening Chronicle, 1997**

Frankie Howerd **Evening Chronicle, 1983**

Ronnie Barker
Evening Chronicle, 1991

Jonathan Miller **The Herald, 1998**

Alan Whicker at a book launch in Newcastle in 1985. He thought the nose wasn't quite right but promised to hang it in the toilet.

James Bolam **The Journal, 2000**

Heather Mills **The Journal, 2008**

Tim Healy **The Journal, 1998**

Kate Adie **The Journal, 1998**

Jimmy Nail **The Journal, 2000**

Alun Armstrong **The Journal, 2000**

Des Lynam **Sunday Mail, 1999**

Robson Green **Sunday Mail, 1998**

Rowan Atkinson **Sunday Mail, 1998**

Hugh Grant **Sunday Mail, 1999**

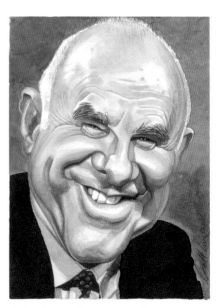

Clive James **Sunday Mail, 1999**

In the late 1990s I produced some cartoons for The Herald newspaper in Glasgow and many caricatures for its sister paper the Sunday Mail. The caricatures were used on the TV page, and because they only needed one a week I could take my time and used the opportunity to develop my watercolour technique.

In those days most of my work for the Newcastle papers was in black and white. Being able to produce paintings to a high level of finish was a luxury and on the whole more enjoyable for me as a water colourist than the constraints of the daily job.

Jack Charlton, enjoying a favourite pastime. **Evening Chronicle, 2001**

Calista Flockhart **Sunday Mail, 1999**

Cameron Diaz **Sunday Mail, 1999**

Clint Eastwood **Sunday Mail, 1998**

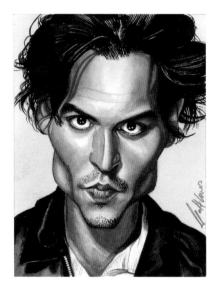

Johnny Depp **Sunday Mail, 1999**

Jack Nicholson **Sunday Mail, 1998**

I've drawn members of the Royal Family many times over the years and this has given me the opportunity to explore family characteristics as well as the aging process.

Princess Ann **Sunday Mail, 1998**

Prince Philip **Sunday Mail, 1999**

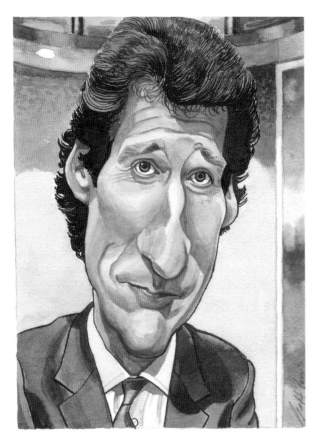

Jeremy Paxman bestowing one of his pitying looks in his role as question master on University Challenge.
Sunday Mail, 1998

Cherie Blair, nuff said! **Sunday Mail, 1998**

stadium rock

MUSIC FIGURES A LOT IN MY LIFE and is one of my great pleasures. Over the years I've played guitar and keyboards in a number of bands. Mike Jamieson, then the Evening Chronicle's jazz and blues columnist, played blues harmonica and we would often practice songs at home.

In March 1988, the Jumpin' Hot Club was running a blues gig in the basement of the Bridge Hotel just by the High Level Bridge in Newcastle. A photographer friend of ours at the Evening Chronicle who occasionally played guitar with us, Denzil, said that we were good enough to perform publicly. Then after a photographic assignment at the Jumpin' Hot Club, he told us that he'd got us a gig there.

Mike had the bright idea that if we performed it would make a good feature for the Chronicle. He had never played in public, I had very limited experience and this would be my first time singing. We sat through the first set getting more and more anxious, then, to our horror, just as it was our turn, in walked Ray Stubbs 'King of North-East Blues'. Great!

Mike played harmonica, I played guitar and sang, but what we hadn't noticed until we stepped up was that there was only one microphone. So I had to hold the guitar up high while Mike hunched over, none of which helped our jangling nerves. We did half a dozen songs receiving more than just polite applause, probably because they couldn't hear us, and Mike got plenty of material for his feature.

Evening Chronicle, 1988

In the 1980s some of the top rock bands played concerts at St. James's park and other North East venues. The Evening Chronicle brought out special supplements to celebrate the shows. I did caricatures of the bands for the supplement covers and gained extra inspiration by opening the window next to my desk to listen to them rehearse during the afternoon before the concert.

The Rolling Stones
Evening Chronicle, June 1982

Up-to-date photos of Bob Dylan were rare at the time and didn't give me enough information to make a reasonable caricature, so I did a portrait instead for his appearance at St James's Park. **Evening Chronicle, July 1984**

Bruce Springsteen, the Boss.
Evening Chronicle, June 1985

Queen's Freddie Mercury. **Evening Chronicle, July 1986**

David Bowie **Evening Chronicle, June 1987**

Status Quo, another good excuse to draw guitars.
**Evening Chronicle,
June 1988**

Local lads made good.
Clockwise from below: Hank Marvin,
Bryan Ferry, Neil Tennant, Brian Johnson,
Mark Knopfler, Sting.

Jimmy Nail, without his crocodile shoes. **The Journal, 1996**

Liam Gallagher **The Journal, 1990s**

Mick Jagger. Why struggle to draw smooth-faced young pop stars when you have subjects like this? **Sunday Mail XS magazine cover, 1999**

football heroes

FOOTBALL HEROES INCLUDE players like
Jackie Milburn, in action, right, drawn
for the cover of a special Evening
Chronicle tribute, and below at his desk,
writing his own sports column.

The Pink, 1983

Evening Chronicle, 1988

Malcolm MacDonald (who played for NUFC 1971-1976) was asked in an interview what his ambition in life would be. He replied that 'it would be lying in a hot, foaming bath, smoking a large cigar and holding a gin and tonic, with Barbra Streisand sitting at the other end singing to me'. **The Pink, 1982**

Gary Speed **The Pink, 1998**

I spent many years drawing caricatures for The Pink, the Evening Chronicle's Saturday sports paper. A wide range of sporting stars were interviewed while visiting the North East and their profiles carried alongside the drawings. As you would expect, Newcastle United and Sunderland footballers appeared often, beginning in black and white in the 1980s and changing to full colour in the 1990s. A lot of the originals were framed and presented to the footballers.

Shay Given **The Pink, 1998**

Andy Cole, painted for **Viz** *magazine and printed on T shirts. In a shock move in 1995 Newcastle United's goal scoring favourite Andy was sold by manager Kevin Keegan to Manchester United.*

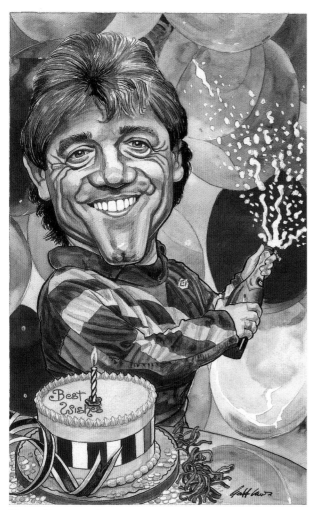

Kevin Keegan. This painting celebrated Kevin's first year as Newcastle United manager. **The Pink, February 1993**

Peter Beardsley, from a series of posters painted for **The Pink** *in the 1994-5 season.*

Caricatures of footballers like Gazza would sometimes be used in the papers when their lives became more newsworthy.

I wasn't keen on the footballers' fad for perms, a nightmare to draw, and I was much happier when shorter hair came back into fashion.

Bobby Robson during his time as NUFC manager, 1999-2004. **Evening Chronicle**

Paul Gascoigne, painted for a special feature at a time when Gazza was recovering from his knee operation and sometimes found himself at a loose end. **The Journal, 1991**

Les Ferdinand, originally painted as the **Evening Chronicle** *Goal of the Month prize and presented to Les, below. The version on the right was painted for an exhibition.*

*Alan Shearer leads Newcastle United to a
Wembley cup final.*
Evening Chronicle, 1988

The unfeasible banner

In early 1993, before the revamp of St James' Park, Newcastle supporters made a huge banner featuring my 'magpie' cartoons, which they would unfurl and hold above their heads in the stands. Someone thought it would be a good idea to make an even bigger one to completely fill the Leazes End so they could listen to the match rather than watch it!

Newcastle United fans and their banner, 1993.

Northern Arts were going to fund this new banner and asked me to design it. The idea was that I would meet a group of hardcore supporters to discuss the elements that they would like to see on the banner and incorporate them into the design. We had several meetings in The Strawberry pub (where else?) and the ideas flowed with the pints. Eventually a design was agreed and, amazingly, it seemed it really might happen.

How, and where, I could actually paint a banner 240ft x 150ft in size was something I hadn't considered. It was at this point that reality kicked in and health and safety became an issue. The Fire Brigade insisted on the banner being fireproofed and this would have made it too heavy to lift. Where could it have been stored between matches? After several months of madly unrealistic optimism the whole project collapsed.

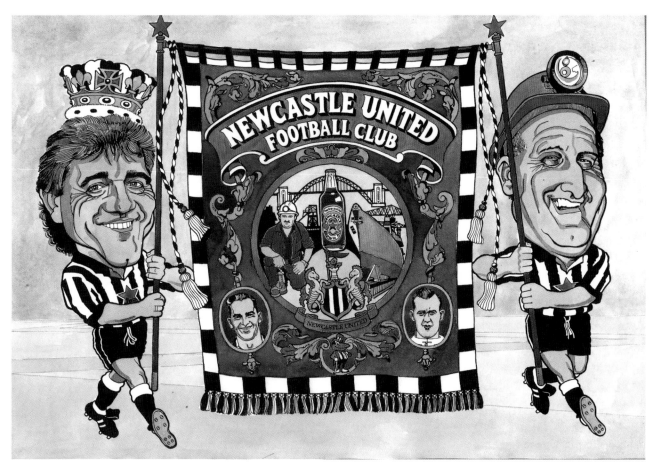

The design for the impossibly huge banner. With Kevin Keagan, Sir John Hall, Jackie Milburn, Hughie Gallacher, the magpie and other local icons.

Jack the Mag

From 2001 through to 2006 I did a cartoon called Jack the Mag, in collaboration with Paul Tully, for the Newcastle United programme. Paul was the publications editor for NUFC and he would ring me with ideas for the next cartoon.

We'd discuss the ideas and decide which one to use. Some of the best jokes had to be discarded in order not to upset the club and the supporters.

I would do the drawing and email it to him, which was a darn sight easier than the days when I used to rush down to the Red Star delivery office at the Central Station with a big envelope of drawings to send to London for the next day's Daily Mirror.

Jack the Mag lasted nearly six seasons before financial restraints at NUFC led to its demise.

It was good fun, I enjoyed playing around with the stereotypes which didn't seem to have come very far since Andy Capp's time. Over the years the North East's flat cap and whippet image has gradually faded away as Newcastle has emerged as the party capital of Europe and a vibrant 21st century city.

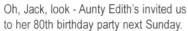

politics

Harold Macmillan drawn in the late 1970s for my own amusement.

I did caricatures of Maggie in a number of guises when she first became Prime Minister. I liked the contrast between the big soft hair and the variety of ways of portraying the hard woman beneath.
Evening Chronicle, 1980

Tony Benn takes on Dennis Healey in a fight for the deputy leadership of the Labour Party.
Evening Chronicle, 1981

Margaret Thatcher's and Ronald Reagan's 'special relationship' returned to its pre-Falklands War bickering in the winter of 1982.
Evening Chronicle, 1982

Arthur Scargill, leader of the miners and Mrs Thatcher's bitter enemy, leads the Welsh miners into a strike in support of health service workers.
The Journal, June 1982

Margaret Thatcher and the disastrous Poll Tax. **Evening Chronicle, 1990**

Margaret Thatcher and Michael Heseltine. One of the many battles between them just before Mrs Thatcher was ousted from Number 10. **Evening Chronicle, 1990**

In 1993 Swan Hunter's ship yard in Wallsend was struggling to find orders and was threatened with closure. The Evening Chronicle ran a campaign to try and prevent the closure and I did a full-page caricature of the prime minister, John Major, in the guise of Lord Nelson unable to see the sinking Swan Hunter's ship. The headline ran ... NO JOBS, NO MONEY AND NO FUTURE.

The page with the cartoon won the UK Press Gazette Certificate of Merit 1993.

The caricature was used by the workers of Swan Hunter, printed on T-shirts, and sold to help raise a fighting fund in their fight to stop the closure.

John Major, I See No Ships.
Evening Chronicle, 26 May, 1993

The Save Our Swans campaign, studiously ignored by the Tory Party conference of October 1993. Swan Hunter were hoping for a new buyer but only Tynemouth MP Neville Trotter and Stockton South MP Tim Devlin turned up for a fringe meeting at the Blackpool conference out of 154 invited Tory MPs. Others were attending a briefing by the Bingo Association of Great Britain instead. **Evening Chronicle, 13 October, 1993**

budget day

Nigel Lawson. **Evening Chronicle, 1987**

Every budget day from the Thatcher years through to Gordon Brown The Journal would use one of my cartoons on the front page. We would listen to the chancellor give his budget speech in the House of Commons then discuss the main features and decide what would be the headline story. I would then translate that into a cartoon, usually featuring the chancellor in some way.

Because of the timing of the Budget speeches, cartoons for the Evening Chronicle had to be done the day before and required a degree of inspired guesswork. Those for the Journal were done the evening after the Budget speech and appeared the following day.

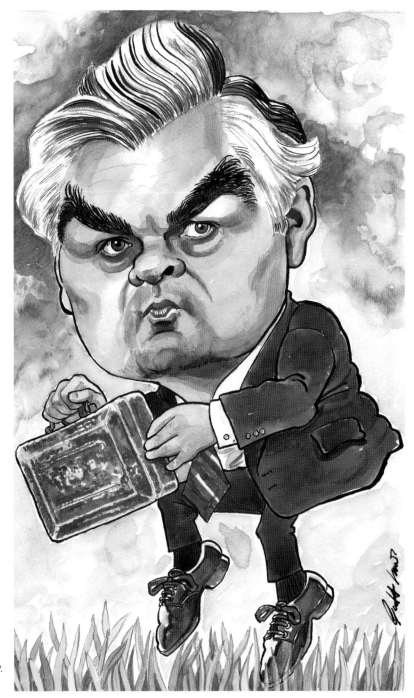

Norman Lamont, treading carefully.
The Journal, 1992

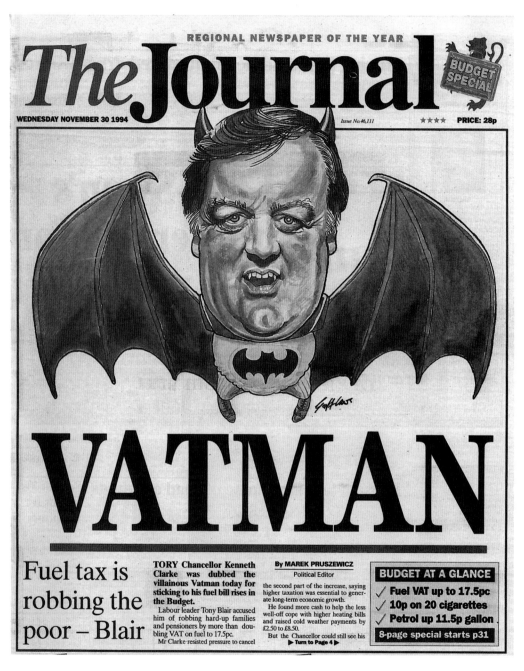

Ken Clark was recognised amongst cartoonists as being quite a difficult subject to portray. The jowls and general chubbiness perhaps. As Wally Fawkes said 'It is harder drawing round people than thin ones'. Clark's extrovert character and tendency to perform meant he had a different look with every changing mood.

Ken Clark as Batman headlining the Budget fuel bill rises, 30 November 1994. This one featured in the British Press Awards for that year.

Cautious Ken's balancing act. Ken Clark treads a cautious line between vote-catching and belt tightening in his pre-election budget.
**The Journal front page
November 27, 1996**

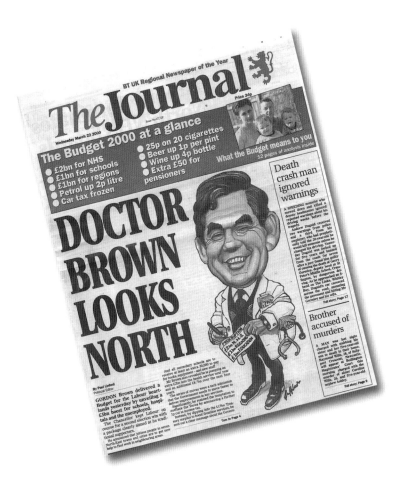

Chancellor Brown delivers cash to the North East.

The Journal Budget Special March 22, 2000

I won!

Phew! John Major as boxer celebrating his victory over
John Redwood in the Conservative leadership elections.
The Journal front page July 5, 1995

Top dog Bill Clinton wins the US election beating Republican Bob Dole to become the first Democrat to win a second term in fifty-two years. The Journal printed a special edition at 4am to be the first on the streets with the result. A copy was sent to the Clintons at the White House.

Caricatures of George Bush and Bill Clinton in winning poses were prepared for the Evening Chronicle prior to the presidential elections of 1993. Clinton was then used in the Chronicle on the day of the results. The same was done for the General Election of 1992 with Neil Kinnock and John Major. The losers were never used.

The Journal front page, November 6, 1996

John Major, Tony Blair, Paddy Ashdown, general election results. **The Journal, May 2, 1997**

Politics and the Paul Linford column

Paul Linford writes…

'Shortly after I became political editor of The Journal in January 1997, editor Mark Dickinson asked me to start writing a weekly 1,000-word column for the paper. It would have its own page, the centrepiece of which would be an illustration by Geoff Laws. I would liaise with Geoff each Friday morning about the subject matter for the cartoon, and so began a partnership which was to last more than a dozen years. Some of those conversations with Geoff would be over very quickly. He or I would have an idea, we'd both agree it was a good one, and off he went to put together his image.

Sometimes, however, the discussions went on for ages, as we both struggled to get our heads around how we were going to illustrate the impact on the North East of the local government area cost adjustment or some other arcane Whitehall funding formula – although we invariably got there in the end …'

Members of Parliament vote by a large majority to ban hunting with dogs, but will it become law?
29 November, 1997

If the idea was unresolved by the end of our conversation I was left to mull it over. I found from painful experience that staring at a blank piece of paper while the hands of the clock moved ever closer to the looming deadline was not the best approach. That way panic lies and that doesn't get the job done. So I'd often have a little wander to the coffee machine and invariably ideas would pop into my head from nowhere.

I still don't understand the process but once one idea comes then, like buses, more usually follow. I would imagine the scene in my head moving it around like a film director trying to get the best angle, work the ideas up in rough, phone Paul and we'd choose a favourite. Paul wasn't keen on using captions or speech bubbles so the drawing always had to be self explanatory within the context of the article. The most difficult were those where he was putting forward concepts with no particular politicians to caricature. Hopefully our conversations would be over by about 10am and that left me about three hours maximum in which to gather up reference photos and do the drawing. Simple!

It was the most difficult and stressful time of the week for me but it kept me on my toes and made me think.

Stephen Byers is mentioned as a possible candidate for the post of Official Government Spokesman. In reality, a human shield for Tony Blair. **14 February, 1998**

*William Hague
lurches to the right.*
2001

Paul continues...

'... Geoff produced some great images in the course of those twelve years. John Prescott features as a bulldog in many the cartoons – albeit one which ultimately slunk away with its tail between its legs following the defeat of his regional assembly plans in 2004.

As for Tony Blair, his teeth were invariably portrayed as so gleaming white. It was sometimes hard to see where each one began and ended.

Probably my favourite was the then Tory leader William Hague with his Doc Martens, union jack T-shirt and I Love Maggie tattoo after his 'lurch to the right' in 2001, although Geoff was probably helped by the fact that Hague is a natural skinhead.

As I wrote in my column when Geoff left The Journal, they say a picture is worth a thousand words, and since that was the average length of the column, the old adage was never more apt than in the case of the long-running Linford-Laws partnership.

Looked at as a whole, these cartoons constitute no less than a pictorial history of North East and UK politics from 1997 to 2009 – the ascendancy of Blair followed by his long, slow fall from grace, the struggles of Gordon Brown for the succession only to find it was a poisoned chalice.'

The Liberal Democrats under Charles Kennedy target Tory seats in an attempt to become the real Opposition party. **28 September, 2002**

Bank of England Governor Eddie George when asked whether he thought lost Northern jobs were an 'acceptable' price to pay to curb inflation in the South East had no option but to agree.
24 October, 1998

Tony Blair apparently determined to frustrate Prescott's most cherished aims in transport and the North Assembly. **3 July, 1999**

Is having the Queen read out the Government's programme at the State Opening of Parliament a tradition worth holding on to? Or is it better for her to declare the whole thing open then let the politicians get on with it? **20 November, 1999**

North Tyneside MP Stephen Byers' ministerial career is de-railed by a row over his spin doctor Jo Moore, who said that 9/11 was a very good day to bury bad news. **20 October, 2001**

The regional prosperity divide between the North and South remains unbridged. **3 November, 2001**

A hundred and twenty-two Labour MPs rebel against what they see as Blair's rush to war. After years and years of loyal and often grudging obedience, the Labour Party is finally reasserting itself. **1 March, 2003**

While the government can talk about tackling regional economic disparities till the cows come home, it is not prepared to put its money where its mouth is. **13 September, 2003**

Mr Brown told the commons that he was publishing
'for each region of the country full employment plans'.
He didn't. **13 December, 2003**

SCOTCH MIST

FULL EMPLOYMENT PLAN FOR THE NORTH EAST

North Tyneside MP Stephen Byers argues that the new manifesto should be Blairite rather than Brownite in tone.
8 May, 2004

Labour loses Newcastle to the Liberal Democrats in the local elections and Labour leader Tony Flynn loses the job he has held for ten years. **12 June, 2004**

The referendum on regional assemblies in the North West and Yorkshire is postponed while the poll goes ahead in the North East. **24 July, 2004**

Tony Blair speaks at the Sage Gateshead with Alistair Campbell once more at his side. The headline for the piece says –
'Spins, smears – and the maybe the odd policy'. **12 February, 2005**

In the run-up to the General Election thoughts turn to the forthcoming wedding of Prince Charles and Camilla Parker Bowles. **5 March, 2005**

Former Health Secretary, Darlington MP Alan Milburn decries the Tories' use of individual patients to draw attention to the failings of the NHS under Labour. **12 March, 2005**

Doubts were cast on Tony Blair telling the whole truth about Weapons Of Mass Destruction and his having seen Jackie Milburn play as a child. **30 April, 2005**

The day of Live 8, and the eve of the G8 summit in Gleneagles at which the future of Africa will loom large. **2 July, 2005**

David Blunkett is forced to resign for the second time after an administrative oversight, while Blair steers New Labour towards the rocks. **5 November, 2005**

John Prescott's 'integrated transport policy' was a disaster and his dream of a network of regional assemblies finally ran into the sands in the previous November's North East referendum. **26 November, 2005**

Prince Charles involves himself in issues of political controversy. **25 February, 2006**

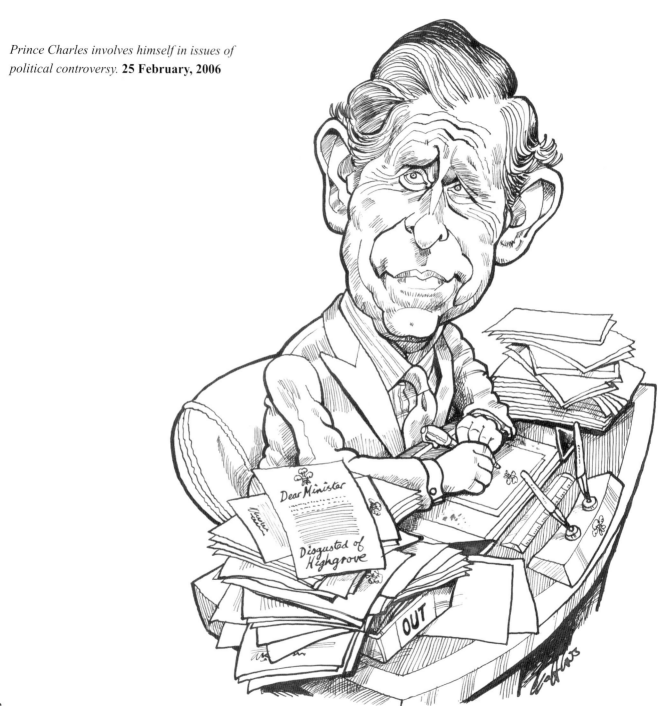

South Shields MP David Miliband decides not to run for the Labour leadership despite the increasingly desperate entreaties of the Anyone but Gordon brigade. **21 April, 2007**

Gordon Brown needs to restore public trust in Labour by acknowledging his own past dependence on spin.

28 June, 2007

Three weeks after Gordon Brown becomes Prime Minister opinion polls give Labour a lead over the Conservatives in the so-called 'Brown Bounce'. **21 July, 2007**

Following Tony Blair's handover to Gordon Brown and a series of mishaps, Labour's fortunes take a downturn.
22 December, 2007

Chancellor Alistair Darling struggles with the Northern Rock crisis, the double U-turn over the taxing of 'non-doms' and the reforms to capital gains tax. **16 February, 2008**

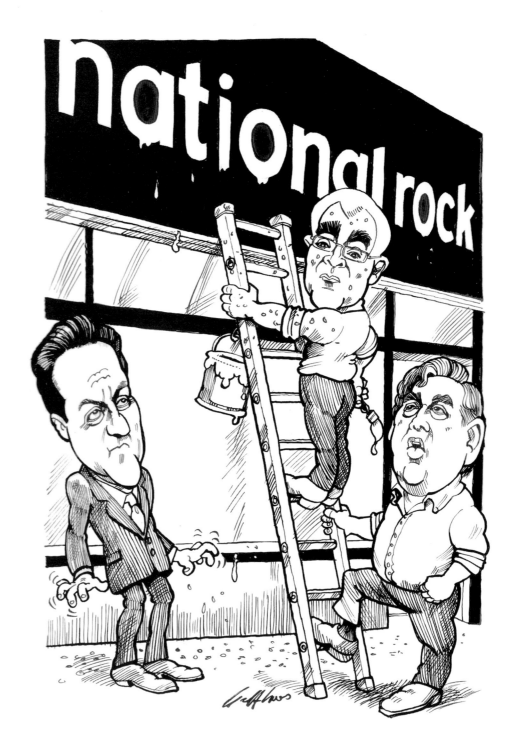

The Northern Rock crisis deepens as it is taken into public ownership.
23 February, 2008

Labour suffers disastrous losses in local elections.
3 May, 2008

Tyne Bridge MP David Clelland has a minor spat with a constituent and is one of 171 MPs who vote to keep the discredited system of MPs' allowances.
5 July, 2008

South Shields MP David Miliband is considered as a possible challenger to Gordon Brown as leader of the Labour party. **2 August, 2008**

There is speculation as to who David Miliband might have in his cabinet should he become Labour leader. North East Blairite Alan Milburn is named as a possible chancellor. **9 August, 2008**

Chancellor Alistair Darling delivers a Pre-Budget Report in the face of a severe economic downturn. **29 November, 2008**

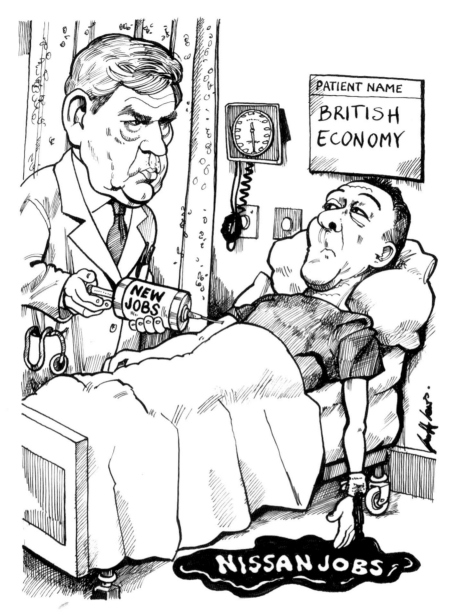

PATIENT NAME
BRITISH ECONOMY

NEW JOBS

NISSAN JOBS

The Prime Minister produces a package designed to create 100,000 new jobs but there is still the baleful prospect of a million UK job losses in the next twelve months. This was my last cartoon for the Paul Linford column and rather apt considering the circumstances. **10 October, 2009**

other stuff

IN 1999 I WAS APPROACHED by Ozzie Riley of the North East based Dodgy Clutch theatre company to sculpt caricature heads for giant figures for Newcastle's millennium celebrations. I'd never done anything remotely like that before but I thought I'd give it a go. I made the heads of local heroes Alan Shearer, Jimmy Nail, Sting and Bobby Thompson. So began a long association with Dodgy Clutch, and an opportunity to practice those dormant three-dimensional skills I learned at college.

The Bus of Fools was commissioned by Newcastle City Council as part of the 2001 New Year's Eve celebrations and consisted of an open top double decker bus full of cartoon characters from Viz magazine flying over the Theatre Royal. It was over thirty feet high. I loved the way it was supported only on its rear wheels.

The Bus stood in front of the Civic Centre for three days up to 31 December 2000 when it was lifted on to Barras Bridge and ceremoniously set on fire. The idea came from the enormous sculptures which are burned in the squares of Valencia every year. One arm of the Fat Slag is the only piece to survive.

We went on to create some complicated large-scale projects and although I did the designs and a lot of the practical work myself I couldn't have managed without the help of Jon and Adam with their technical know how and amazing creativity and skills in the workshop. Thanks also to the rest of the Dodgy Clutch team for their support, bacon sandwiches and coffee.

Larger than life caricature sculptures of the Krape Twinz used at the Hexham Festival 2003. The real Krape Twinz, left, are musicians and the sculptures were used as part of a performance they gave with Dodgy Clutch at the festival.

This life size sculpture of man playing a 12ft grand piano in the lake at Saltwell Park was created for the Gateshead Festival 2003. Like the Bus of Fools I enjoyed making the sculpture look as if it was defying gravity. At intervals music came from the piano, the lid lifted and water sprayed from a fountain inside. The piano figure was also used at the opening of the Sage Gateshead.

This caricature sculpture of Pavarotti was created for the opening of the Sage in December 2004. The figure skated round and round on an ice rink while singing Nessun Dorma!

I'm very fortunate to have had a job that I've enjoyed and that has been so fulfilling.

To be faced each day with a blank sheet and produce something that was new and unique was immensely rewarding. It wasn't about the pay cheque.

Working for an organisation that published newspapers every day, I was allowed free reign in what I produced.

The fact that I turned up for a day at the office wasn't a problem to me. I thrive on working to deadlines and the office environment gave me the structure to complete the work on time.

Left to produce any work of my own at home I suddenly discover a deep interest in cutting the lawn, reading a book or newspaper even a bit of hoovering, anything other than drawing. Give me a deadline and it's done!

And, as a colleague once said to me, 'Relax mate, it's just tomorrow's chip wrappers …'